MW01708719

The George Jay School
1909

. . . a glance back at
elementary public school education.

Bob Warren

with photographs by

Bob Gretsinger

Canadian Cataloguing in Publication Data

Warren, Bob, 1946-
George Jay School 1909

Includes bibliographical references.
ISBN 1-895332-19-2

1. George Jay School -- History. 2. Education, Elementary--British Columbia--Victoria--History. I. Gretsinger, Bob. II. Title.
LE5.V5W37 1998 372.9711'28 C98-910818-X

Production by:
Desktop Publishing Ltd.
Victoria, BC

Printed by:
Premier Printing Ltd.
Winnipeg, MB

Book ordering:
Bob Warren
1118 Princess Ave.
Victoria, BC
V8T 1L3

Contents

Principals of George Jay Elementary

1. H.B.MacLean 1910 - 1915

2. Harry Charlesworth

3. T.W.Hall

4. Arthur T. Hunkin

5. Norman Forbes 1937 - 1940

6. William McMichael 1940 - 1951

7. Reginald McKay
   Richard James (acting)

8. Cyril Michell 1955 - 1968
   Donald Inkster (acting Sept.- Dec. 1968)

9. A.I. (Les) Isaacson 1969 - 1970

10. James Ellis 1970 - 1982

11. Garnet Jackson 1982 - 1987

12. Robert Tubman 1987 - 1991

13. Brian Wile 1991 - 1994

14 Mary Hendy 1994 -

With thanks . . .

. . . to the countless staff, students, and parents, past and present, that contributed so much information and expressed such interest in the book, that the project seemed all the more worthwhile.

Thanks also to teacher Bob Gretsinger for photography work. All pictures in the book including school, city archives and provincial archives have been retaken and developed in the George Jay School photography lab. Teacher Kathryn Bergstrom was a very willing helper with proofreading. Her love of history and genealogy made her a natural choice to ask for help in this area. Thanks to Marj McMillan for help with cover design and suggestions in many areas of the whole project. Her "practical McMillan method" really pays off.

A big thank you to the Parent Advisory Council for helping to fund the project. Their hard work and dedication enables us to undertake many projects at the school, which help to make the school experiences of the children much more interesting and meaningful.

The whole process of first time publishing has been most interesting and enjoyable thanks to the expertise and suggestions of Jim Bisakowski of Desktop Publishing Ltd.

The annual school photograph of the building – circa 1922 – a tradition carried on today.
Note the horse drawn buggies on Princess Ave. (School Archives photo).

George Jay

On the afternoon of December 9, 1910, The George Jay Elementary School was officially opened. A formal ceremony was held in the assembly hall which was crowded with parents and students. The principal of the new school, Mr. H.B. MacLean accepted the keys to the building from the chairman of the School Board, Magistrate George Jay, whom the school had been named after. Among the distinguished guests who listened to the congratulatory speeches were His Honour, Lieutenant Governor Paterson; Alexander Robison, B.A., L.L.D., Superintendent of Education; School Board Chairman George Jay and school trustees; Hon. Abraham Smith, American Consul; and Rev. Stevenson of the Emmanuel Baptist Church.

Students had been in attendance at the new school since September. Construction had begun the previous year in 1909 to meet the needs of the rapidly growing community in the Spring Ridge / Fernwood area. Magistrate Jay must have felt very pleased as he took part in that opening ceremony so many years ago. Here was a man who had done a great deal to further the interests of education in Victoria.

George Jay was born in Norwich, England on August 26, 1860. In 1870 he arrived in Victoria with his mother, following the trail of his father who had been lured to B.C. by the prospect of the Cariboo gold rush. As a young boy, George attended the Boys' Central and Collegiate schools. Pursuing his interest in law, which would lead to a distinguished career, he articled for Edwin Johnson's law firm and after being admitted as a barrister he formed a partnership with J. Stuart Yates.

George Jay's interests were many and varied. He had been active in the militia, holding a lieutenants commission in the No. 1 Company, Victoria Rifles. He was a member

Mr. George Jay, 1860-1940, a strong advocate of the importance and value of education. (school archives photo)

of the crack shooting team which won various shooting matches in the 1880s. Magistrate Jay enjoyed sports all his life, either as a player or as a spectator. As a young man he especially enjoyed rugby, playing on local "rep" teams who would arrange matches with the navy. In years to come, in his position as Chairman of the School Board, he "gave every encouragement to the development of the game (rugby) in the schools of the city, for he knows its part in physical welfare and in character formation."[1] His interest in music was evident as he was a valued member of Victoria's famous Arion Club Choir for many years.

When George Jay retired in good health at age 75, he left behind a record of public service that had rarely, if ever, been equalled in any Canadian city.

In 1901 the young lawyer was elected as a trustee to the City School Board. Thus began a life of public service which would last until his retirement in 1936. In 1905 he was appointed stipendiary magistrate to small debt court. In 1907 George Jay was appointed stipendiary magistrate of the County of Victoria and in that same year he was appointed police magistrate of the City of Victoria. Acceptance of this office was on the special request of Sir Richard McBride, who was then the Premier of the province. In 1908 he was elected Chairman of the School Board, a position he would hold until he retired in 1934.

George Jay's interest in young people was obvious throughout his distinguished career. It was through his efforts that a juvenile court was established in 1910. He was one of the driving forces behind the establishment of Victoria College. "A great believer and a great supporter of better education, Magistrate Jay has always done his part to give education a chance."[2]

Noted for a most retentive memory, Magistrate Jay could "sit back in his private room and tell of hundreds of cases, each a story in themselves, never forgetting a detail." When he retired in good health at age seventy- five on August 26, 1936, Magistrate Jay left behind a record of public service that had rarely, if ever, been equalled in any Canadian city.

It was fitting then, on that December day back in 1910, that Victoria's newest school should be named after a man who had, and who would continue to do so much for the youth of this city.

1 Victoria Daily Colonist Newspaper August 28, 1936
2 Victoria Times Newspaper, July 11, 1936

H.B. MacLean

It is always exciting to start a new year of school. That first day back each September is special for both students and staff. The rooms and hallways look so clean and shiny; the children so keen and ready to begin. It must have been especially so in 1910 with The George Jay School being brand new. The principal, Mr. H.B. MacLean, was fairly new to Victoria, having arrived just the previous year.

Born June 12, 1884, at Mount Herbert, Prince Edward Island, he began teaching in a one room ungraded school at Cascumpec, P.E.I. in 1901. Mr. MacLean recalled his first class. "There were 35 to 40 youngsters in all grades. Some were French speaking with no English. I was 17 - terrible. I got $225.00 for that first year of teaching. That was perhaps more than I was worth. They offered me an extra $10.00 a year if I stayed. Best compliment I ever had."[1] After a number of postings Mr. MacLean moved to Victoria in 1909. Since he first began teaching Mr. MacLean had taken an interest in handwriting. In a letter to his fiancee in 1909 while he was an assistant principal of South Park School he wrote: "I see quite a lot of progress in some things, especially their writing and homework."[2] On July 14, 1910, Mr. MacLean and Mrs. MacLean were married. His wife May had been his "star pupil" in his class of 1905. She recalled Henry's fine penmanship in his letters and she was especially fond of a lovely pen Henry had sent for her 17th birthday in 1907.

---

1 Vancouver Province Newspaper. Oct. 29, 1970. p.39

2 Ibid

Mr.H.B. MacLean showing proper style for good penmanship (school archives photo)

The H.B. MacLean Method of Handwriting was used across Canada (B.Gretsinger photo)

In 1915 Mr. MacLean was appointed principal of the new Normal School. The school was located at Lansdowne and Hillside, and is now part of Victoria's Camosun College. Mr MacLean noted that in 1915, this area seemed to be "well out in the country." It was the following year when he transferred to the Vancouver Normal School that complaints of poor handwriting began to be heard. Pupils graduating from elementary to high school were required to write entrance exams. Papers were marked by inspectors at Victoria. Dr. S.J.Willis, Superintendent of Education in Victoria was dissatisfied with the writing of pupils all over the province. Dr. Willis appointed a commission to study the problem and make recommendations. Mr. MacLean was chairman of that commission. The group worked for a year and a half looking at text books of all English speaking countries and consulting with representatives of numerous different systems.

A result of the commission's work was the H.B. MacLean Method of Handwriting, which was introduced into all schools in B.C. in 1921. Writing and printing manuals were supplied free to all students in the province with separate manuals for each grade of the elementary schools and a senior manual for high school use. Certificates were presented for each grade. The primary certificate was awarded "for sitting in a healthful position, for holding the pencil correctly, and for doing good print writing."

Mr. MacLean stayed at the Vancouver Normal School for the next 33 years, teaching natural science, school gardening and handwriting. His system of handwriting became so well accepted it spread all over Canada. Many of us today recall the endless lines of figures and letters that were necessary to achieve Henry's maxim; "practice makes perfect."

Although Mr. MacLean did not like to be called a "handwriting expert", there can be no doubt that he was. Federal, provincial, and municipal police have called on Mr. MacLean for over 50 years to examine questioned documents such as forged wills, threatening letters, etc. He could cite many examples of how handwriting evidence determined the outcome of trials. For example, the murder case in which three anonymous letters from the suspect had misspelled words. The suspect misspelled eleven of those thirteen words on the witness stand.

The longest serving textbooks in British Columbia's educational system were handwriting texts written by Mr. H.B.MacLean.

As a hobby Mr. MacLean was an amateur magician. He enjoyed entertaining and gave many performances for crippled children, senior citizens and other similar groups.

In fine health during his 88th year, Mr. MacLean came back to visit The George Jay School in 1972. He was the honored guest at the opening ceremony of the new gymnasium.

The Early Years

The first decade of the twentieth century was one of rapid population growth in Victoria and Vancouver. The Klondike gold rush of 1898 had generated immigration, and real estate speculation was on the rise. Building construction in urban areas was progressing at a tremendous rate and exploration of resources was adding to the boom. During this period Vancouver surpassed Victoria as the most populous city in the province.

The enrollment in B.C.'s public schools was increasing dramatically during the early years of the 20th century. The percentage of regular attendance was also increasing each year. The 1901 Public School Act made schooling for children, 7 to 14 inclusive, compulsory if they lived in a city district. Truant officers did their best, but in some cases, parents were anxious to have their children working. In 1909, while The George Jay School was under construction, Victoria Superintendent of Schools, Edward B. Paul, stated that a truant officer had been assigned "to attend to the many cases of absenteeism in the schools and the result has fully justified his appointment. Several cases of parents' neglect to send their children to school have been brought before the Police Magistrate."[1] Magistrate Jay, with his keen interest in education, would not have been sympathetic to a parents explanation of truancy.

Because of the rapid population growth; if the compulsory education laws were strictly enforced, the schools in some areas would have been terribly overcrowded.

1 Annual Report of the Public Schools of the Province of B.C. 1909-1910. p.39

A shortage of trained and experienced teachers was a problem in B.C. during this period. Many vacancies were filled by educators from eastern Canada. Samuel J. Willis, the principal of Victoria High School and College 1908-1916 (and Superintendent of Education for B.C. 1919-1945) was from P.E.I. as were many involved in education in Victoria at the turn of the century.

"Most elementary schools in Victoria, so it seemed, were led by Campbells from Charlottetown: Earnest at Sir James Douglas, his brother John M. at North Ward, and Allison (not related) at South Park. Over at George Jay, Spud Islander Henry B. MacLean was devising his MacLean's Method of Handwriting, scourge of many a non-conformist schoolchild yet unborn."[2]

By 1903 the streetcar system reached up into the Fernwood area. (British Columbia Archives photo)

As mentioned, the early years of the century saw tremendous growth. In 1890, Victoria had become only the third city in Canada to have an electric streetcar system. This introduction of public transportation would have an impact on residential growth in certain areas of the city. By 1903 the streetcar system reached up into the Fernwood area

2 Come Give A Cheer. p.39

and by 1905, with its own line, the Fernwood area was a fully recognized community. 1907 had seen more construction than any year in the city's history with 349 new buildings. The long awaited opening of the C.P.R. hotel, The Empress, was on Jan. 20, 1908. There were approximately 3100 residences in Victoria by the beginning of 1907. By the end of 1913 there were over 7600. To keep pace with home building, massive street paving projects were undertaken and some sixty miles of concrete sidewalk were laid. Fernwood Road was paved and sidewalks were put in during the year. During 1909 the city employed an average of 900 workers per day at an annual cost of over $600,000 in wages. By 1911 the work force increased to 1,137 per day and the payroll increased to over one million dollars for the year. In 1909 the city pipe yard was built at the south east corner of Chambers Ave. and Queens Ave. Sewer lines were constructed in the area of the new school along Princess Ave. from Vancouver St. to Chambers Ave.

The building boom continued into 1910. Building permits, which had totalled only $363,580 in 1900 had risen to $2,373,045 in 1910. Lester and Frank Patrick prepared to build an artificial ice arena in the city; work began on the new Union Club. Plans for an elaborate new drill hall on Bay St. were drawn up. Caught up in the excitement of the building boom carpenters began asking for $4.50 per day.

The Horticultural Class - 1914 (School Archives photo)

There were now 4200 telephones in the city and the road to Mill Bay, though uncompleted, was now passable, and was christened the "Malahat Drive". Teachers at the new school would not believe that 85 years from then, the principal of The George Jay School, Brian Wile, and other staff members, would commute daily to work from Mill Bay over the Malahat Drive. Building permits for 1911 totalled $4,026,315. By 1912 the police department had their first motor vehicle and the fire department was becoming motorized.

By 1912 compulsory education included municipalities and by 1921 all children over age 7 and under 15 in all of B.C. were required by law to attend school. To help ensure that boys and girls received minimal education, and to help enforce compulsory attendance, the

1921 Employment of Children Act was passed. This act denied males under 14 and females under 15 employment in primary and secondary industries. Certainly it was a step in the right direction.

It seems more and more parents were realizing the importance of their children receiving an education. This view plus the growing population and resulting increased enrollment meant for bigger and better schools being built. The George Jay School was built at a 'healthy time' for education in B.C. By 1910 education accounted for the single largest segment of the provincial budget with $745,742.00 out of $7,738,257.00. During times of economic prosperity money is available for expansion and building of new schools. Conversely, during tough times, cuts have to be made somewhere, which is a pattern for public education in B.C. during the 20th century.

In 1909, the first truant officer for Victoria was assigned to attend to the many cases of absenteeism in the schools.

1909 -The Building

Had The George Jay School been built just a few years earlier, or even a few years later, it probably would not have been built on such a grand scale. The schools' beginning was at a time of elaborate and expensive prewar school construction. The development of the Victoria school system after 1891 became the responsibility of the municipality rather than the provincial government. The development and growth of the Victoria school population and buildings was orderly and measured, except for the boom years 1908-1914. The economy was very good and the growth in the population of school age children was tremendous. In 1903 and again in 1904 Victoria ratepayers had defeated school board proposals for the building of new schools. It wasn't until 1908 when classroom space was drastically needed that voters approved the new school to be built on Princess Ave. The construction of The George Jay School would be followed by the building of Sir James Douglas School in 1910.

School boards could choose between using government architectural services or the best of the private architectural firms the city could offer. Either way the government would pay a substantial portion of the cost of the new buildings. The George Jay School was designed and constructed in the popular Edwardian style by the architectural firm of C. Elwood Watkins and Thomas Hooper. Built of brick and concrete, it was the first building in Victoria to be constructed with reinforcing steel. The contracting company was a local group; the Parfitt brothers of Fernwood. The five brothers; Aaron, Albert, Fred, James and Mark, were responsible for constructing many local landmark buildings. Some of their more noteable projects included the Bay St. Armory, the Fernwood United Church, the James Bay Hotel, and Christ Church Cathedral.

Built of brick and concrete, George Jay School was the first building in Victoria to be constructed with reinforcing steel.

The George Jay School was built at a cost of $75,000. The eleven classrooms, administrative office and assembly hall covered 33,112 square feet. Such was the population explosion that it wouldn't take long before this grand new building was overcrowded.

In his annual report, E.B.Paul, the Superintendent of Schools in Victoria notes that in 1911 there had been an unprecedented increase in school enrollment - one almost equal to the total increase for the previous eight years. The attendance figures for The George Jay School for January 1912 show a total of 394 students in 10 classes. Two of the classes had 49 students each, and many had 40 or more pupils. In the first year of operation two temporary classes had to be opened to help accomodate the increase in the school population. One class was in the basement and the other was in the assembly hall - both temporary and unsatisfactory makeshifts. A new six room schoolhouse in the Oaklands district was under construction in the fall of 1912. This was to relieve the overcrowding of The George Jay School. Throughout the city the school accomodation was insufficient and overcrowded conditions prevailed.

A typical elementary school classroom (British Columbia Archives photo)

In his report of November 1912 for the school year 1911-12, George H. Deane, Inspector of Schools for B.C., was concerned that not enough was being done for the elementary schools. He points out that the majority of school children receive their education in the elementary schools. 110 of last years' elementary school students went on to high school, but 337, though still residing in Victoria were not attending high school. Inspector Deane was concerned that so much money was to be spent on the new Victoria High School when conditions in elementary schools needed improving.

Conditions at the new George Jay School were much better than in other areas of the city. Inspector Deane was disappointed that teaching was still taking place in basements, in rooms badly lighted and ventilated, and in such buildings as those in use at Hillside, Spring Ridge and Rock Bay. He hoped that all schools, not just the new ones, would have up to date furniture and equipment. His report indicated that many schools were badly in need of an adequate supply of dictionaries, maps, globes, and other appliances. "It astounded me to find that 23 divisions teaching geography had no servicable globes."[1] It is interesting to note that Inspector Deane found the "teachers conscientious, painstaking, and working hard for the advancement of their pupils. In a number of instances the classes were in

Div. III - 1923
Photo courtesy of Clara Burns (nee Renouf)

1 Public Schools Report for Province of B.C. 1911-1912, page 30

charge of experienced teachers who had excellent control and did very effective work. But in striking contrast to these were a few whose work was wretched."[2]

The problem of overcrowding became so bad that a number of classes in the district were held in tents during the 1913-14 school year.

"The worst of the overcrowding was removed in 1914 - 15 when the city's prewar building program reached fruition with the completion of four large elementary schools and a massive new high school (Vic. High). These elementary schools, while of permanent brick construction, were relatively inexpensive and functionally styled two-storey structures. They reflected a relative decline, under population and financial pressures, in the architectural standards of Victoria's schools following the completion of the George Jay School in 1909."[3]

Thus The George Jay School was the last of the schools built on a 'grand' scale. The schools of the future would tend to be either the more economic wood frame structure or plain two-storey brick buildings. The one exception to the trend for more modest school construction was the Victoria High School. As The George Jay School was well into its first year of operation, workers three blocks away were hauling gravel and soil out of the excavation site by horse and wagon. This huge 34 classroom building would not be completed until 1914.

The George Jay School was the last of the schools built on a "grand scale". the one exception to the trend for more modest school construction was the Victoria High School.

2 Ibid.

3 Report on building of Victoria's schools

The First Year

At the commencement of school, a student monitor rang a handbell calling everyone in. The students lined up - girls on one side and boys on the other - and marched into school while another child hoisted the Union Jack. Actually there were two bells rung to begin the school day. The first bell called all the students to line up and the second bell was the signal to begin marching in. Former student Jack Leonard still chuckles at the thought of the Milliken boys who lived next to the school yard in the old house on the south east corner of Princess St. and Chambers Ave. The Millikens would rush breakfast and then run to school after the second bell and catch the tail end of the line marching in. They did this for years which was always good for a laugh for the other kids - a good way to start their school day.

In 1910 the average monthly salary for teachers was $83.65

The school day often began with the teacher inspecting each child for nits, clean hands and fingernails and possession of a handerchief.

Teachers would often have a few students do exercises at the blackboard while the rest of the class worked at their desks or watched for mistakes. There was a great emphasis on reading, writing with your right hand and arithmetic. During the early years of the 1900's the curriculum had been relatively narrow, with an emphasis on the "3 Rs". In a response to be more progressive, the curriculum broadened. By the time The George Jay School opened, students were offered a lot more. The "new education" included courses in health and hygiene, physical training, home economics, manual arts, technical education and rural science.

The first year in the grand new school was a busy, productive one. The opening ceremony in December had been an outstanding event. "An excellent programme of speeches, together with songs, chourses and drills by the scholars, was rendered, the entire event being a milestone in the history of city schools[1]." The first staff consisted of H.B.MacLean Esq. principal, John Spouse, Mrs Menkers, Miss J.MacLeod, Mrs Coady-Johnson, Miss S.Hiscocks, Miss E.Dalby, Miss E.Andrews, Physical Instructor, Ian St.Clair Esq.; Supervisor of Drawing, Miss Mills; Supervisor of Needlework, Miss Boorman; and Supervisor of Music, H.J.Pollard. Teachers' salaries for that first year totalled $8,344.28. The average monthly salary was $83.65. Janitors' salaries for the year were $875.00 and substitutes salaries for 1911 were only $58.50. Expenditures for supplies such as writing and drawing paper, ink, pens, pencils etc. totalled $241.86

Miss E. Dalby - Taught at George Jay 1909 - 1929
Photo courtesy of the Dalby family

In the annual report of the Supervisor of Art, it was noted that "at Easter we had an exhibition of the district art work at The George Jay School, during the Provincial Teachers' Convention. This was much appreciated by the visiting teachers, especially by the teachers from the country districts."[2] Student needlework was also exhibited at the Convention. In the annual report of the Supervisor of Domestic Science it was noted that a Miss Preston was appointed to the George Jay Centre which started classes in October. The report noted that the George Jay Centre was small and had no chimney, so that all cooking had to be done by gas.

The report of the Building and Grounds Committee noted that repairs and improvements made in 1911 included raising a chimney, plumbing in the domestic science room, toilet repairs, roof repairs and fencing. The domestic science programme was not readily accepted by all. Many mothers looked upon it as "a fad without raison d'etre, as they consider that they were as competent as the Domestic Science instructors to teach their daughters to cook and sew."[3]

The annual report of the Supervisor of Physical Training (Ian St.Clair - George Jay) makes for interesting reading. He visited every school at least twice a week and gave instruction in physical training to all pupils in attendance. Ian was pleased that in the first year not a single

1 Victoria Daily Colonist, Dec. 10, 1910 p.3
2 Annual Report of the Board of School Trustees - Victoria, Dec.31,1911 p.53\
3 Ibid. p.27

piece of apparatus employed was missing or damaged. His report for the following year notes the continued good work, as there was not one pair of crutches in evidence amongst the 4000 children who attended district classes. The George Jay School won a district championship in its first year. In Girls' Hockey, (field hockey) the George Jay team, winner of the trophy in 1911 and also for 1912, lead from the start, and during the season were not scored against. It was noted that the St. George's School (private school) had to withdraw from the league due to an outbreak of contagious disease.

As early as 1912 the first call arose for the need for a gymnasia at The George Jay School. It would be 60 years before that gymnasium would be opened. Fittingly enough, the guest of honor at the opening ceremony in 1972 would be Mr. H.B.MacLean. In the spring of 1912 a district school basketball league was organized by Mr. MacLean. Over the years to come, The George Jay School would represent itself well, winning many city championships in basketball.

In the fall of 1911 the George Jay Manual Training Building was built. This one storey brick structure was built on the site of the present day gymnasium at a cost of approximately $3500. The annual report notes that the Board should take the George Jay building as the model for future Manual Training Schools. Manual training courses had become quite popular. In their second and third terms of woodworking the boys were taught to make useful models such as bookstands, hatracks etc.. These projects involved using earlier operations such as glueing, dowelling, etc. that the boys had learned. Some teachers in 1911 felt they were expected to do too much. The manual training instructors' report "strongly recommends the Board to appoint a man to grind tools, sharpen saws, repair benches, etc. in our centres, leaving the Manual Instructor free to teach."[4]

In the spring of 1912, the first district school basketball league was organized by H.B.MacLean, the principal of George Jay.

The George Jay School was one of the first schools in the province to have a school garden. For many years, the enclosed area on the south side of the building was used as a garden plot. Every year it was dug and planted, giving students the opportunity to raise vegetables, and to plan and lay out a garden. Produce was sold and proceeds were given to the Red Cross during the war years. Later the proceeds would go towards school activities. Eventually there was a heated greenhouse where bedding plants were raised. A Mr. Bennett looked after the greenhouse, the school borders, and class window boxes. He was so successful with these activities that the school board appointed him as head gardener for the system.

4 Annual Report to the Board of School Trustees Dec. 31, 1912 p.33

Manual Training courses (woodworking) were popular. British Columbia Archives photo

In 1913 the Agricultural Instruction Act was passed. The B.C. program was headed by John Wesley Gibson. Food production was even more basic than the 3 Rs. It was hoped that rural students would see the importance of their parents' occupations and that city students would appreciate the land and work involved that produced their daily bread. "By 1918 there were 7,630 students enrolled in school gardening in the province."[5] In time this program was to be phased out for various reasons. Problems such as vandalism, marketing, and summer care would often cause setbacks. The post-war depression and resulting funding cuts eventually led to the discontinuance of the program.

The first few years were very productive for the new school, but they were not without problems. A few of the problems arose from neighbouring activities. The city dog pound was located across the street from the school on Chambers Ave. The pound housed up to 100 stray dogs and teachers at times would have to compete with the noisy neighbours. In a letter to the Times Newspaper on June 27, 1911, Mr. MacLean mentioned how the dogs would greet all new arrivals at the pound with a chorus of barking. It wasn't long before the pound was relocated. Next to the pound on Queens Ave. from Chambers Ave. up to Spring Road was the city pipe yard. The daily hammering and banging was

5 Annual Report of the Public Schools of B.C. 1918 p.54

Proud students admiring their gardens (School Archives photo)

another distraction which would eventually be relocated. At the same city yard was a building used to transfer garbage that was collected in the area. Horse drawn garbage trucks (one horse wagons) would have their loads tipped into larger four and six horse wagons at the city collection building. The larger wagons would haul the garbage to the harbor where it would be loaded on to barges to be then dumped into the ocean. Another neighbouring concern was a cattle slaughter yard located north of the school towards the Oaklands area. In his June letter to the newspaper, Mr. MacLean says " I have seen horned cattle being chased through the school grounds by cattle pound employees, and running mad among hundreds of little children in the midst of their play."[6]

Of a lesser concern was the Lion Saloon on the corner of Queens on Chambers Ave. A proposed city bylaw of the day would buy out the saloon license for $4000. Eventually the saloon closed and the building later became The Lion - God is Light Sunday School. A family photo taken in the 1920s in front of the Sunday School shows Mrs. Josiah Manton and children standing in front of the double doors of the old saloon.

The George Jay School was one of the first schools in the province to have a school garden.

It is interesting to note that the name for the Fernwood area came originally from the Fernwood Manor. Built in 1860, the fifteen room mansion was the first stone house built in the colony. Built for Benjamin W.Pearse, who had purchased some 300 acres in the area, the manor was named after the natural vegetation and foliage found in the area. This area

6 Victoria Times Newspaper. June 27, 1911

Basketball Team - 1920. Torrie Rennie,Margaret & Mabel Harris, & Clara Renouf (front) The girls would catch the No.3 Trolley to play at South Park and North Ward Schools. Teachers did not have cars in those days.(Clara Burns Photo)

had at first been called Spring Ridge, because of the natural springs found in the area. One of the two main springs was found just east of The George Jay School. The springs had been a source of public water supply for many years. By 1866 the Spring Ridge Water Co. had been created and hollow wooden water pipes served the growing community. By 1875, Elk Lake water was being piped to the city. The natural spring waters in the area eventually attracted breweries which claimed the pure waters produced excellent beers. One of the breweries was the Lion Brewery which opened a Tap Room - the Lion Saloon, on the corner of Queens Ave. and Chambers Ave., which is now the city owned playground adjacent to the schoolyard.

No Shortage of Wood. 1920s and '30s

Educational happenings in Victoria during the 20s were a reflection of the provincial scene. During the early 20's school populations continued to rise rapidly. The increased costs that the municipal taxpayers had to bear was resulting in more and more public dissatisfaction. In 1924, Premier John Oliver's Liberal government commissioned a survey of the province's educational system. The commission was headed by George M. Weir, professor of education at U.B.C., and J.H.Putman, senior inspector of the Ottawa schools. The survey, which became known as the Putman-Weir Survey, made recommendations, some of which promoted new concepts in education. The most important recommendation was the establishment of the junior secondary school for grades 7,8, and 9. The junior secondary school would be able to offer more subjects to students at a time when they would be considering vocational choices. As well as the basic subjects, students were offered home economics, manual arts, music, art and commercial subjects. The report also suggested that special "opportunity" classes be established in each large elementary school. These classes would accomodate slow learners. When Central School was turned into the first junior high school on Vancouver Island, Mr. Hunkin left the principalship of George Jay School to become the first principal of the newly-organised junior high school. Mr. N.P.Forbes took over the principalship of George Jay School. George Jay became the first school in the Victoria district to have pupils from grades one to six only.

1930s This was the period when community sport and recreational centres were built in many areas across the province to provide an outlet for unemployed youth.

Former student Jack Leonard(Victoria's Mr.Pennyfarthing) with son Chris and grand daughter Elizabeth - three generations of George Jay students (B. Gretsinger photo, Nov. 1997)

In an article in the "Islander" section of the Times Colonist newspaper, neighbourhood resident Phyllis Van Hoeke recalls her days at George Jay in the late 1920s and early 30s. At that time classes were grade 3 to 8 and graduating students went on to Vic. High. It was shortly thereafter as mentioned, that junior high schools were introduced. The home economics room was equipped with many two burner gas plates. The sewing classes used treadle sewing machines with round bobbins made by White. Students from nearby Oaklands and Quadra schools would walk down once a week to use the George Jay facilities for their household training. At the back of the school Mr. Goldfinch taught wood working in the work shop building, or Manual Training building as it was known. It was a small brick building, probably 25 feet by 40 feet, which matched the main school building. It was one large room and had wood working, two- vice benches. These benches were adjustable for boys of different height. According to former student Jack Leonard, shop teacher Mr. Goldfinch could throw a mean piece of chalk to bring students back to reality should any start to daydream or fool in class. Scraps of wood from the shop probably found their way to the school boiler. Mrs. Van Hoeke remembers well " two very long stacks of four foot fir wood at the back of the school for the boiler; the heating plant of the

Army cadets on parade circa 1921.
Victoria City Archives photo

building. No shortage of wood in the 1920s. The pile never did diminish and must have been replaced on weekends or after school hours, as we never saw a truck or horsedrawn cart"

Mrs Van Hoeke went on to state that she was "sure that boys and girls that went to school in 1929 and 1930 would agree that school life was rather rigid and not very colorful. The main purpose of the elementary school was to teach reading, writing, and arithmetic. Other basic subjects were art, health, geography, history, some physical education and recreation - which was on a very low profile." Things have certainly changed. Although the story of education in British Columbia is one of change, - some things remain the same. Teachers driving students to inter-school competition is the same today as it was seventy-five years ago. Mrs. Van Hoeke reminised about riding in Mrs Todd's model T to play baseball against South Park and other schools and how a lot of the kids wanted to ride with Mr. Wilfred Johns when he bought his new convertible with the rumble seat. She remembered the $600.00 price tag being a considerable sum for a new car. In the '90s the students would look forward to riding in Mr. Gretsinger's "Lamborgreeni", a large green Ford station wagon, or Mr. Lansdell's speedy red sports sedan.

Div. 10 - 1928.
All dressed up for picture day
(School Archives photo)

During the late 20's the effects of the depression became more widespread. B.C.,with its resource based economy, felt the effects. Public attention turned to the cost of educating the youth of the province. Programs launced a few years earlier were curtailed and teachers' salaries were reduced. The average salary in 1931 was $1800 per year; by 1934

George Jay award winning drill team - 1920s
(School Archives photo)

Division 7 - 1933
(School Archives photo)

the average salary was $1300. Teachers didn't always receive a sympathetic ear from the community. Many unemployed workers resented their complaints because they felt teachers were lucky to have jobs. Parent - Teacher Associations began fund raising for their schools, supplying free milk and hot lunches to students, and providing sports equipment and library books. In March,1932, Joshua Hinchliffe, Minister of Education in the Conservative government was suggesting city and municipal councils prohibit school boards from offering courses in manual training, domestic science and such which some now felt were "fads and frills." The government now with a debt of well over $143 million appointed a committee to look into the financial affairs of the province. The chairman was George Kidd, a Vancouver businessman, and the report came to be known as the Kidd Report. The report recommended spending cuts in many areas but most drastically in education. It went so far as to suggest that students should begin work once their elementary schooling was complete. Criticism of the report came from all areas of the province. The pendulum of educational funding continued to swing.

The Liberal government of Duff Pattullo in 1934 under the slogan "work and wages" won a record number of seats. G.M.Weir was appointed Minister of Education and Provincial Secretary. The depression and funding shortages was not to affect education. The age limit of free education was raised from 15 to 18 or until the completion of grade 12. It was hoped high school courses would keep students in school until completion and even draw back other young people who had dropped out. This was the period when community sport and recreational centres were built in many areas across the province to provide an outlet for unemployed youth. Again though, increased services meant higher costs, and in June 1934 Mr. Weir set up a commission on School Finance. H.B.King was an adviser to that commission. Following the King Report, as it was known, the government began to consolidate the many small school districts into larger units.

The Minister of Education announced a complete revision of the curriculum in every grade. Part of the curriculum revision of the 30's was the introduction of the "unit" system. Subjects in the Elementary school were organized on broad topics or "units." It was hoped subjects were meaningful to children. To help meet this end, and to avoid an over emphasis on text book use, the use of audio-visual aids was encouraged. Schools were provided with projectors and films and film slides became the "progressive" way to present a lesson.

Schools were provided with projectors and films, and filmslides became the "progressive" way to present a lesson.

It was hoped schools would teach co-operation rather than selfish competition. Ideas that would resurface with more widespread support in decades to come. By the late 30's, "the main preoccupations of educators became once again the perennial ones of finance and the provision of increased vocational and technical training."[1]

1 Wilson,J.Donald, Schooling and Society in 20th Century B.C. p.113

The Baby Boom - 1940s -'50s

In 1973 legislation made the provision of kindergarten mandatory for all school districts. This legislation officially recognized what had been taking place for years.

In September of 1944 Victoria's first kindergarten for 5 year olds opened at Spring Ridge School. This first class was very successful and by 1946 there were 8 classes.

The Department of Education's first Kindergarten Manual in 1954 states that the "purpose of the kindergarten year is to ensure the maximum growth of each child, physically, socially, emotionally, as an individual and as a member of a group." The kindergartens were very popular and much in demand but again were another drain on finances. The post war baby boom, when they reached grade one age, put a greater demand on the existing school space. Any space for new kindergarten classes would have to be built at considerable cost. The number of classes in Victoria remained at eight until the early 60s.

By the end of the 1960s there were 98 school districts in the province.

The early 1950s saw attempts to broaden the curriculum in Victoria schools. The 1952 annual report for District #61 indicated that increased attention was being paid to secure personnel who had qualifications in music, physical education, art, and to a lesser degree, dramatics and folk-dancing. The 3 "R's" still comprised the backbone of the school programme but these others were important. Parent - teacher interviews were becoming popular in most schools. The interviews were to supplement the regular form of reporting to parents.

Junior Basketball Champs - 1949 British Columbia Archives photo

In 1952 there were eleven special classes for handicapped children in the Greater Victoria schools. Four special classes for slow-learning children were held at George Jay School and two were held at Central Junior High School. George Jay at an early age became the school in District #61 to house special classes. A central location and available space were deciding factors, although the extra space would soon diminish. In addition to the six special classes for slow learners in the district there were two special English classes at North Ward School for New Canadians, and three special remedial classes for pupils who were too handicapped educationally to attend regular classes.

The Department of Education is continually examining, reviewing, and revising the aims and functions of public school education. In September of 1954, a Provincial Curriculum Advisory Board was formed to act in an advisory capacity to the Ministry of Education. The board was composed of people from business, industry, agriculture, labour, the teaching profession and other groups in the province. One of the first jobs of the board was to help prepare the "Aims of Education in B.C." schools which stated that schools are established for "the primary purposes of developing the character of our young people, training them to be good citizens, and teaching them the fundamental skills of learning necessary for further education and adult life."[1] The official "Aims of Education in B.C." also noted that the school was not wholly responsible for educating the youth of the province. The home, the church, the community, and the school should work together to help guide young people. The idea of the community sharing some of the responsibility for educating our youth would resurface at different times over the years.

The full impact of the "baby boom" began to be felt in Victoria in the mid-1950s. Accommodation continued to be taxed to the limit, resulting in the conversion of auditoria and basement space into classrooms and in the formation of large classes, 63 of which contained 40 or more pupils each. Such was the growth in student population that a 'shift system' was introduced in September,1954, at Cloverdale, Doncaster, McKenzie Avenue, Oaklands and View Royal elementary schools.

In December of 1954 voters were asked to authorize the School Board to borrow $3,129,000 under a school loan bylaw referendum. Approval was passed and the Board began an ambitious building programme. New schools included Colquitz Junior High, and elementary schools at Glanford, Gordon Head, Macaulay, and Marigold. Schools having additions built because of overcrowding included Doncaster, George Jay, Margaret Jenkins, Oaklands, Strawberry Vale, View Royal and Willows Elementary; and Esquimalt and Mount View High Schools. Small schools began to be developed by assembling portable units at Lake Hill, Hampton Park and Richmond Road. By the end of the following year, of only six special classes in the district for slow learners, four would be housed at George Jay and two at South Park.

With 3 universities and seven regional colleges to be developed, 1963 was a landmark year for education in B.C.

In January of 1958, the government of B.C. appointed a Royal Commission to examine the educational system of the province. The commission was to pay particular attention to programmes of study and pupil achievement. The chairman was to be S.N.F.Chant, Dean of Arts and Science at U.B.C.. The Chant Report, as it was to be called, made many recommendations. As part of the Chant Commission of 1958 public school kindergartens in the province were surveyed. In Victoria, of the 1,950 five year olds, only 880 or 40 percent attended kindergarten. The Victoria Kindergartens were working on an alternate week basis in which children attended five sessions every other week. From 1963-1965 more classes were opened bringing the number of schools with kindergartens to 17. By 1970, 28 different schools had kindergarten classes.

1 Annual Report of Ministry of Education 1954-'55, p.28

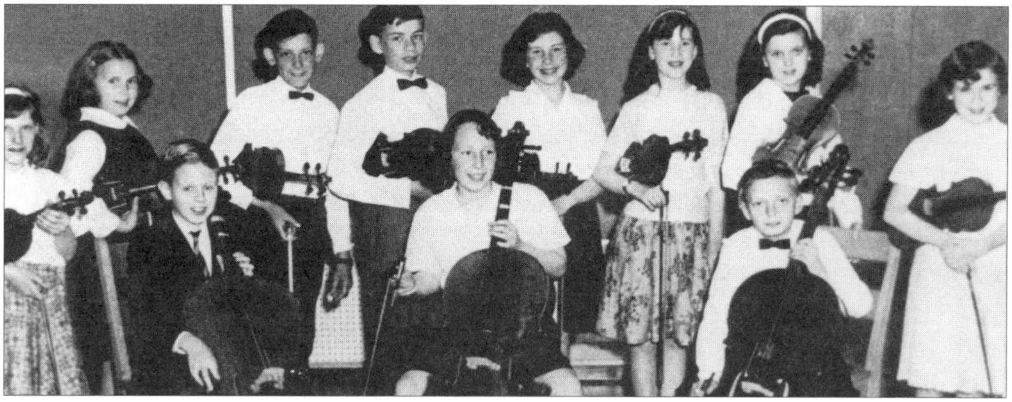

Students enjoyed increased attention to the Fine Arts. Top - Dance, Center - Music, Bottom - Drama. (School Archives photo)

Under Dave Barrett's N.D.P. government of 1972 and under the leadership of Eileen Daily, the Minister of Education, all parties gave unanimous support to the question of kindergartens, and the legislation of April '73 was passed . The concept of pre school education in kindergarten had been accepted. The problem had been in gaining concensus that kindergarten was essential and so should be funded as part of public education.

The Minister of Education, Leslie Peterson, announced in February 1961 , that the Chant Report would be adopted in principle. Parts of the Report would be implemented right away and other areas would receive further study. The big change affecting elementary schools was the transfer of grade seven to the elementary school. This was done where classroom space was available. The new grade seven classes would no longer have Home Economics and Industrial Arts as part of their curriculum. All grade seven pupils would be required to write final exams in June, the results to be used to determine whether students passed or not. There was soon an increase in the number of summer schools provided by local school boards. Students faced final exams and the possibility of summer school before going on to Junior High School - talk about incentive for grade sevens to "hit the books." By the end of the 1960s there were 98 school districts in the province - 73 were municipial districts and 25 were rural districts.

Div. 13 - 1958 - the Annex building is still in use. School Archives Photo

As the baby boom of the mid '40s moved through elementary and high school it was recognized that higher education needs would not be met for the 20% of students who could profit from university education. Following the report of Dr. J.B.Macdonald, the Universities Act was passed by the Legislature in March 1963. B.C. would now offer higher education in three facilities: the University of British Columbia, the new University of Victoria and Simon Fraser University. As well, amendments to the Public Schools Act provided for the establishment of regional colleges. The Legislature passed a separate act to provide for the first church supported university in Western Canada, Nelson's Notre Dame University. With three universities and seven regional colleges to be developed, 1963 was a landmark year for education in British Columbia.

From Boomers to Ballpoints

The 1960s saw the implementation of recommendations of the Chant Report of the Royal Commission on Education. The report made mention that in the modern age of T.V. and movies we were rapidly becoming a nation of spectators and so in the area of physical development of the student, more emphasis should be placed on participating, actively doing, and not viewing. The Chant Report recommended that textbooks be not so copiously illustrated with pictures that the literary or informative value of the text is impaired.

The principal of the 1960s at George Jay School was Mr. Cyril Michell. Here was a man whose career in education was most interesting. Mr. Michell's first teaching position in 1924 was short lived. His class of 20 students of all grades in a one room school at Sandspit in the Queen Charlotte Islands was closed due to a measles epidemic just before Christmas. While in Victoria on holiday he heard of a teaching job at Harewood near Nanaimo. After finding a substitute for Sandspit he took the new job. "A year and a half later he became one of B.C.'s youngest principals when he was named to that post at Brechin."[1] In 1929 Mr. Michell moved to the Victoria District as principal at Strawberry Vale. After principalships at McKenzie, Tillicum, Tolmie, South Park, Beacon Hill, and

The field in front of the school was covered in red cinder, an experiment which was a nightmare for the custodial staff.

1 Victoria Colonist Newspaper. March 5, 1967.

James Bay, Mr. Michell moved to George Jay in 1955. He took "particular interest and pride in the school's four classes of New Canadians - young people from 6 - 18 who have just arrived in Victoria from wide ranging foreign lands."[2]

Mr. Michell had the pleasure of having his daughter, Mrs. Beverly Forward, as a member of his staff. Mrs. Forward went on to teach intermediate students for 22 years at the school and after her retirement would come back as a valuable volunteer in the school library for many years.

Mr. Michell was principal at George Jay until he passed away suddenly in 1968. He is remembered each year at the school when the Cyril Michell Sportsmanship Award is presented to a deserving senior student at the annual year end assembly. Making the year end awards assemblies much more meaningful are the guests that help with the presentations. Mrs. Forward with the Sportsmanship Award; George Jay's grand daughter, Mrs. Healy, with the George Jay Citizenship Award; and Mrs. Thomas and daughter to present a grade six citizenship award in memory of their son and brother, Dave Thomas, a grade six teacher.

The newly introduced ballpoint pen did not necessarily translate to new improved handwriting for students.

Ruth Colman has seen her teaching career come full circle. Ruth began teaching grade two at George Jay from 1964 until 1968. At that time our present day parking lot was occupied by four houses, two facing Cook St. and two facing Princess St. Ruth enjoyed arriving at work and admiring the "beauty of the southwest entrance with stained glass panels above the doors." At that time the field in front of the school was covered in red cinder, an experiment which was a nightmare for the custodial staff. The little flower beds at the front of the school were enjoyed by the entire community. On rainy days the play space in the basement was a busy spot.The play space was missed when that area became rooms 101 and 103 . Ruth recalled how busy Principal Michelle could be. "When I really needed Mr. Michelle to help me with a grade two boy who could not read, I got advice from Amelia. (colleague Amelia Mobey) 'Go to his office before school. Ask if you could talk with him. Go into his office and close the door.' I followed instructions and was greeted with "You're not pregnant, too, are you?" Apparently two other women had recently used the same advice."[3] After teaching at other Victoria schools, Ruth would finish a wonderful career with kindergarten at George Jay in the '90s, retiring in 1998.

---

2 Ibid.

3 Memories of George Jay. Ruth Coleman. 1997

Students are bused to District special programmes housed at George Jay.
(B. Gretsinger photo - 1997)

An article in the August 5th, 1962 Daily Colonist newspaper entitled, "Handwriting is as important as ever....Even in Atomic Age" stated a quiet 'revolution' was going on in elementary schools in Victoria. The 'revolution' was being fought with the pen and was a cultural revolution to restore handwriting to its rightful place as an art of communication. The recent Royal Commission report on education had found some dissatisfaction with the way children wrote. The introduction of the ball point pen in 1961 meant the days were gone - for schools in Victoria and other parts of Canada - when pen and ink meant the old fashioned penholder, a steel nib, a bottle of blue - black ink, and a blotter to sop up the mess. The newly introduced ball point pen did not necessarily translate to new'improved handwriting for students. As has happened in the past, and will again in the future, the idea of more practice, and 'back to basics' in order to master a subject was the theme of the day. The emphasis on penmanship was once again in vogue.

Looking at the school's record book of staff meeting minutes for the 1950s and '60s shows us again how some things don't change, and that some thankfully do. For a December 1955 meeting under the heading "General conduct in and around school", it was noted that:

a) Children hurry too much.
b) Boys neglect removing their hats.
c) Some girls were wearing slacks in class.

At the December meeting the following year it was decided that if the weather was snowy then girls may wear slacks, but not in class. Former teacher Mrs. Marion Barath

Annual staff photo - 1969 - 1970
School Archives photo

reminisced of the time quite a few years later during the '60s of the time when female teachers first wore slacks to work. A class visit to the firehall was good reason not to wear the required dress and being so comfortable the slacks were kept on all day even when the class returned to school. The next day a second staff member was in slacks and the following day, a third. A new, more practical trend had begun.

Staff meeting minutes for November 1964 show that the fine arts were flourishing at George Jay. The upcoming Spring concert would be held for two nights. Teachers in charge would be Mrs. McKay for drama, Miss Mobey for dance, and Miss Broadhurst for music. The school was soon to receive music appreciation records. Teachers of today would be envious of the fine arts facility the school had in the old third floor auditorium with the large curtained stage with lights to enhance the performances.

By January of 1965 the population of the school had risen to 990. The size of some classes had gotten to the point where not all the desks would fit into the traditional rows. Out of necessity, seating arrangements in some classes were in pairs or groups - a prelude to a new idea soon to come - seating in clusters or pods, which was popular in the new 'open-area' classrooms. Other ideas of this period which began to be mentioned in various reports included: the "discovery" approach to learning; the "levels system" in language arts; continuous progress; and "team teaching", which leant itself to use in the new 'open areas'. A number of districts began to establish resource centres where books, records, pictures, slides, and other teaching aids are available for teacher use.

In the mid 1960s the number of New Canadian or English Second Language classes was on the rise in Victoria as well as elsewhere in the province. On February 15, 1965, these

Div. 19 - 1967 Class of New Canadian Students (School Archives Photo)

new students, as well as all Canadians, had a new flag to pay allegiance to. Parliament adopted the new flag which proudly shows off Canada's national symbol, the 11 point red maple leaf. In 1967 Canada celebrated its centennial, commemorating the 100th anniversary of the Confederation. Students all across the country were working on units of study of Canada's first 100 years. At George Jay, teacher Sylvia Hosie was in charge of the schools contribution to the Centennial Pagent which was to be presented in May. Students in Victoria would learn of Canada's great city of Montreal when it hosted the 1967 World's Fair, Expo '67.

By the 1966-'67 school year the population at George Jay had risen to over 1000 students. With 1,078 students and 127 kindergarten students the school was second in size to Lord Nelson Elementary of Vancouver that housed 1,096 students. By the following year George Jay Elementary would be the largest elementary school in all of British Columbia. With 1,132 students and 119 kindergarten students, George Jay Elementary had almost 100 more students than the number two school, Lord Strathcona of Vancouver, which had 1,047 students. To see the school thirty years later with 350 students, it is hard to imagine how crowded it must have been during the 1960s. Even with a separate recess for primary and intermediate students the playground must have been very busy. The present day staff room was used as a classroom during the '60s, and the two rooms that are now the nurses room and the waiting/rest room beside the office, were the original staff room. Again, even with a split recess, the staff room was very crowded. What is even more difficult to imagine is that the original library was located on the other side of the office. This room which measures no more than 10' by 12' is now the photocopy room. The original library book shelves are still on the walls.

By the 1967- '68 school year, George Jay was the largest elementary school in all of B.C. with 1,251 students.

As the 1960s began with the idea that students should be doing more and viewing less, the end of the decade saw an increase in the use of T.V. as an aid to instruction, particularly through the use of video tapes. By the 1990s television would be looked at in a different light. Statistics show that the average child will spend approximately 28 hours a week watching television, which is more time than they will spend in school in front of a teacher. The same statistics show the average North American child will witness 200,000 acts of violence and 16,000 murders on television by the time he or she is 18 years of age. - An issue for the 1990s ? "Violence on television will be more of a factor in juvenile crime than poverty, race or parental behavior."[4]

4 "Programmed for violence." Times Colonist Newspaper, Oct. 12, 1997. p E3

Population Patterns Change - 1970s

The 1970-1971 annual report by the Minister of Education shows that George Jay school had dropped to the number two position in population in the province. Lord Strathcona Elementary in Vancouver had 1,029 students. George Jay was not far behind with 1,027 . There were 929 students in the main building and 98 at the Annex which housed grade three students. The days of record numbers of students would not last long.

As well as the regular school programs the administration was also in charge of a number of special district programs. Teachers centered at George Jay would work with students in hospital or recuperating at home, as well as with any students receiving care at the Eric Martin Psychiatric Pavilion. Students staying at the Juvenile Home received their instruction through George Jay as did any students enrolled in the Alternate Program. According to principal James Ellis, in the field of education in Victoria, the school was "all things to all people." With such a large population and so many programs involved in the school, the role of the administrator was a very busy one. Things ran very smoothly and efficiently under the direction of principal Jim Ellis who was in charge of the school from 1970 until 1982 when he transferred to Glanford Elementary School. Shortly after the large number of students attending in the early 1970s, the population pattern of the neighbourhood began to change. Neighbourhood maturation coupled with apartment development resulted in the rapid decline of enrollment at George Jay . By June of 1977 the enrollment would be down to 609.

Neighbourhood maturation coupled with apartment development resulted in the rapid decline of enrollment at George Jay School.

Teacher Dawn Powell and her Volleyball Team 1972 (School Archives Photo)

The educational curriculum was under constant revision, with textbooks, films and related teaching aids being revised to keep pace with the curriculum trends. As part of the constant revision, locally developed courses began to be introduced. One example was the Victoria school district's outdoor education course in which George Jay students took part in during the 1970s. - a prelude to the Camp Columbia outings of the '90s.

Declining enrollments in the urban districts did not slow down the rising cost of education.

In school construction, certain patterns emerged during the early 1970s which were related to a drop in enrollment in a number of districts. School boards remodeled and renovated schools to provide a variety of instructional areas from small seminar rooms to new large multipurpose areas. The establishment of library, resource centres in schools was becoming more common. The George Jay school would fit in this pattern. By having the much needed gymnasium built, the auditorium was not needed for physical education and thus able to be converted to the resource centre it is today.

With the crowded conditions at the school in the early '70s, staff and students eagerly awaited the opening of the new gymnasium. Interesting to note that 1971 was the year of the highest number of capital expenditure approvals for gyms (114) and libraries (98) throughout the province. These numbers would drop off over the next few years and more effort would be directed to bring buildings up to current standards for program needs, safety and fire protection. The fire escape towers on the north and south ends of George

A crash course in paddling canoes - Outdoor Education, late 1970s (School Archives Photo}

Jay would be the latest capital expenditure project for the school to date. The ceremony to dedicate the new gymnasium and library resource centre of the school took place Monday evening, March 6, 1972. The guest of honor at the ceremony was the first principal of the school, Henry MacLean, in fine health at the age of 88. When Mr. MacLean first opened the school in 1910 there were six on staff. By 1972, that number had risen to 41; which is very similar to the number of staff during the 1990s. It is interesting to note that for the school gymnasium dedication ceremony, principal Mr. James Ellis sent out invitations to the opening, not only in English, but in Chinese and Punjabi which were also spoken by parents of many children in the school.

Outdoor Education leaders & students - late 1970s Maeva Sundher, Frank Marlatt, Ray Davison, Ollie Goldsmith, Bill MacPhee

Teacher Judy Ashurst & Grade 7s - Outdoor Education Nature Study -late 1970s (School Archives Photo)

With the opening of the new gym and a better place to practice, the boys' basketball team under coaches Bob Kidd and Dave Flannagan won the first of many city championships during the 1970s. Under coach Mr. Maeva Sundher, the boys again won the top prize in 1973. With coach Sundher the boys were among the best in the city for many years to come and won many city championships. The most recent city championship for boys basketball would come under coach Mr. Oliver Goldsmith in the '80s.

One of the provincial highlights of the 1972-73 school year was the creation of the Provincial Educational Media Centre. Administered by the Audio-Visual Services Branch, the Centre would produce film, television, and other media forms to meet specific educational needs. Free collective bargaining between teachers and school boards was established during the 1972-73 year.

The Division of Special Services of the Ministry of Education has a number of areas of responsibility. One is the approval of special education programmes developed by school boards to meet the needs of children with special problems. During the 1972-73 school year, 1,335 approvals were granted for special education programmes by school

Teacher Terry Casey and Div. 2 - 1975 (School Archives Photo)

boards. As integration became more desirable, more programmes were necessary to meet the needs. Where once children were segregated because of 'special needs', school districts were now in the process of integrating all but the most severely impaired into regular schools. By the 1974-75 school year 1,841 approvals province wide were granted. Over 1200 of these were for Learning Assistance Programs. The approvals would allow school districts to deploy additional resources in ways designed to meet the needs of children with learning disabilities. The number of special programmes housed at George Jay during this period enabled the school to help meet the needs of not only the area, but the district as a whole, as many students were bused to the school.

Mr. and Mrs.H.B. MacLean - Guests of honor at the ceremony to dedicate the new gymnasium and library resource centre. 1972 (School archives photo)

George Jay City Champions - 1975. Coach Maeva Sundher (left) and Principal Mr. Jim Ellis (right) School Archives photo.

The teacher and enrolment data chart for 1976 reflects the number of special programmes at the school. With 647 students, George Jay was the largest elementary school in Victoria. The number of teachers (F.T.E.'s) at 43 was almost twice that of the second and third largest schools in the district: Gordon Head at 564 students and a F.T.E. of 24.5, and Oaklands school with 536 students and a F.T.E. of 25.5

In February 1973 a change to Regulation 14 of the Public Schools Act was made by the Minister Of Education , Mrs. Eileen E. Daily. From now on, discipline in every school would be similar to that of a kind, firm and judicious parent but would not include corporal punishment. Judging by the number of entries in the corporal punishment record book on display in the library, there would have been many young scholars who would have cheered that announcement. Considering the strap was given for a great variety of reasons such as truancy, cheating, fighting, disobedience, smoking, swearing and the list goes on, the fact it was used 44 times for the 1969-1970 school year, with the population being as high as it was, shows it was being administered in a judicious manner. It didn't take some youngsters long to get into trouble. In the days preceding Halloween, one student received three on each hand for throwing firecrackers on the way to school. He received his punishment at five to nine before the first class began. Some took more than one visit to learn a lesson. After being in to see the principal a few days earlier, buddies Terry and Bart received 3 on each hand at 1:05 on March 11,1969 for rock throwing, after being warned at <u>noon</u> that

The Centre for exceptional children - 1974, Ray Shergold - co-ordinator (center) with teachers Terry Foreman, Ollie Goldsmith and Marie MacInnes

same day. The underlining for noon is the principal's entry in the corporal punishment book.

Learning the three R's continued throughout the 1970s . A strong staff meant for smooth sailing. Many of the staff members of the day went on to roles in administration at various district schools; among them Terry Casey, Maeva Sundher, Frank Marlatt, Peter Gallagher, Terry Foreman, Lance Foreman, and special class teacher Ray Shergold, to the district office. A highlight of the 1976-77 school year was the establishment of a core curriculum for all schools. Ministry work continued on assessment programs to help monitor student successes across the province. It was hoped the declining enrollments in many districts would enable some de-escalation of rising educational costs. The Special Programs Branch of the Ministry, formerly the Integrated and Supportive Services, was reorganized as a branch of the Schools Department. Realizing that rapidly falling school populations in the urban school districts would endanger resource centres and learning

Wizard of Oz - 1979 - left to right - Cindy Pascuzzi, Lisa Littlechief, Karla Neufeld, Patty Dijak. (School Archives Photo)

George Jay Staff 1972 - 1973
(School Archives photo)

Teacher June Shearer
& Div.18 - 1974
(School Archives Photo)

The gymnasium would be filled wall to wall with science projects during the annual Science Fair - 1970s & '80s (School Archives Photo)

assistance programs, a ratio of one approval (for special programs) for each 350 pupils was adopted.

Declining enrollments in the urban districts did not slow down the rising cost of education as had been hoped. By 1977-78 the budget for education in British Columbia was nearly $1 billion. The emphasis in education would be directed at upgrading academic standards with an eye on the costs. In January of 1978 the newly named Division of Public Instruction would initiate an elementary school accreditation program, as well as a French core curriculum. By the end of the 1970s instruction in metric measurement was being offered.

Future in Miniature - 1980s

"The schools of the country are its future in miniature."

- Tehyi Hsieh - Chinese educator

1980 saw the introduction of micro computers into classrooms on an experimental basis to test their viability as teaching aids.

1980 saw the introduction of micro computers into 100 classrooms across the province on an experimental basis to test their viability as teaching aids. It did not take long to see the potential use of the computer as a teaching - learning tool. Optimism was high regarding the future of computers in education. It was felt that the problem of ensuring an adequate supply of quality courseware and of training teachers to use the computer effectively might impede widespread integration of computer technology into the school system. Researchers felt that "computer assisted learning must be given time to evolve, and that computers should naturally find their place in the education system."[1] Computer education would not come cheaply. From an economic point of view the arrival of the computer was poorly timed. History had begun to repeat itself as unemployment soared and lines began to lengthen at the food banks. Provincial funding for education was drastically reduced. In February 1982 the provincial government presented the public

1 B.C. Ministry of Education Annual Report 1980-1981. p. 74

sector restraint program. Reductions were made in library budgets, curriculum supplies, P.E. programs, computer supplies, performing arts, science supplies, and extra-curricular supplies. In 1983 many teachers and school support staff throughout the province walked off the job for three days to protest the cuts in education funding.

Between 1982 and 1986 the province had seen a number of different education ministers:

1982- Honorable William N. Vander Zalm
1984- Honorable John H. Heinrich
1985- Honorable James J. Hewitt
1986- Honorable Anthony J. Brummet

It was in 1987 that the Royal Commission on Education was appointed under the direction of Mr. Barry Sullivan, Q.C., and hopes were high that stability would return to the educational scene.

In the Royal Commission report, "A Legacy for Learners," Mr. Sullivan points out how complex education has become, and how much faith the people of this province invest in education. British Columbians all over this great province hold strongly to the belief that schools do make a difference in peoples' lives, that they are the social institutions that best prepare us for what lies ahead.

The library boasts the largest square footage of any elementary school library in the province.

Our expectations for schools are high.

"In the broadest sense, we have long expected schools to serve as agencies for civic and democratic development and as places where our culture and values can be sustained and transmitted to the young. We have likewise come to expect that schools will provide custodial care for children and socialize them into certain norms of behavior, as well as prepare and select them for later careers."[2]

We realise the importance of the role of the teacher when we look at

"new expectations that have been appended to the already considerable expectations of the past. Today, we turn to schools to help us enshrine language rights, to preserve diverse cultural heritages, to promote social equality and justice through recognition of individual differences and the integration of special needs youngsters, to provide health education and related services, and generally to co-ordinate social programs and facilities associated with the overall care and nurture of the young."[3]

---

2 "A Legacy for Learners", The report of the Royal Commission on Education. p.7
3 Ibid. p. 8

George Jay Staff 1985-'86 (School Archives photo)

Of the thousands of questions raised during the Royal Commissions inquiry; the one raised countless times, and in countless ways, and the most important single question Mr. Sullivan felt obligated to answer, was: " Can any institution shoulder the social as well as the educational responsibilities we have given the schools and those who work in them?" Meeting both the social and educational needs of such a diverse society becomes the focus of those providing school services in the 1990s. In an essay entitled "The Importance of Teaching", from a Royal Bank of Canada kit on education, it is suggested that if a doctor,

Music teacher Trevor Jones with his proud looking 'strings' group (School Archives Photo)

lawyer, or dentist had 30 or 35 people in his office at one time, all of whom had different needs and some of whom didn't want to be there and were causing trouble, and the doctor, lawyer, or dentist, without assistance, had to treat all of them with professional excellence for nine months, then he might have some conception of a classroom teacher's job. Expectations of the classroom teacher are higher than ever before.

The 1980s were the years the Christmas hamper drive was the busiest. Under the direction of teacher Mary Lane; who exemplified the caring, giving, teacher that the school has seen so many of over the years; the annual hamper drive would collect, sort, wrap, and deliver hundreds of boxes of food, clothing, and gifts to needy families in the neighbourhood. After 43 years teaching; 25 of which were at George Jay, Mary retired, a year earlier than she had originally planned in order that a younger colleague would not be transferred due to declining enrolment. Following her retirement, Mary would volunteer in the school with her beloved grade ones. Marion Cox, a classroom assistant in the school for many years but also retired, now also volunteers on a regular basis. The devotion of so many helps make it a special place.

Health and safety have always been important for staff and parents. Different concerns have arisen over the years causing a shift in focus so that students are aware and informed.

Teacher Mr. MacPhee and District Rugby Champions (School Archives Photo)

Buddies Everett & Thomas and the library totem

In 1918 schools were closed due to an outbreak of Spanish flu. In 1924-25 the smallpox epidemic was news. In the 1940s and 50s the spread of polio was a concern. Schools were threatened with closure in 1947 to stop the spread. In the 1960s sex education for boys and girls was the topic of discussion. Parents and teachers became more aware of the dangers of child abuse. During the late 60s and 1970s the use of drugs became a concern. In 1970 the first Block Home Safety program was set up. In the 1980s and 90s the health issue was AIDS. Young children in some inner city areas have to be made aware of the danger of used syringes left on playgrounds. Staff are made aware of the importance of carefully dealing with all playground accidents or situations such as a simple nose bleed.

As the needs have arisen over the years, special programs have been added. During the first half of the century, programs for students who did not speak English as their first language were sporadic or non existent. During the 1960s teachers, parents and trustees recognized the needs of the ever increasing number of students with English as a second language and programs were added at a tremendous rate. This need continues to be met throughout the province. The English

The largest elementary school library in the province. (B. Gretsinger photo - 1997)

Second Language reception class at George Jay in the 1990s under the guidance of teacher Wendy Pritchard may vary in number from 10 to 15 students from various parts of the world who may speak little or no English. It is always amazing to see how quickly these young students become part of the mainstream of the school.

By the 1980s, schools that had sufficient number of first nations students were able to offer alternative programs to further assist these students in their studies. The Native Indian Students Learning Assistance Program (N.I.S.L.A.P.) at George Jay has been in effect since the late 70s. During the 1980s the program was under the direction of Karin Clarke, who saw the need, and went on to work on curriculum development for first nation students. Teacher Genevieve Gleason and assistant Linda Joseph carried on the program which works on instilling a pride of culture and heritage as well as reinforcing reading, writing and arithmetic. The entire school community enjoyed the project that saw a 15 foot yellow cedar totem pole

Automation of collection of 17,000 books by Marj

carved from scratch in the hallway by the gymnasium over a period of three months. The pole now proudly stands in the top floor library.

The library boasts the largest square footage of any elementary school library in the province. This lovely bright, open area which originally was the auditorium has seen thousands of students pass through its doors, whether on the way for instruction or just a quiet get away to read or play chess. The library is the home of the popular "Read for the Top" contest begun in 1983. Student teams annually vie for the top spot in an effort to win ribbons, trophies and book prizes. The library book collection of 17,000 plus titles is added to each year through school funding and donations from the parent group. Computer automation of the collection in 1990 by Marj McMillan meant easier access and a more efficient borrowing operation for the growing collection. One internet line is available for student research use. More will be added as costs come down.

As the 1970s saw many basketball championships, the 1980s saw a swing to an emphasis on volleyball. Under boys coach, teacher Mr. Jack Lansdell, and girls coach, teacher Ms. M. Kavanagh, numerous appearances in city finals were the result of hours of practice time in the well used gym. The seasons capped off with the championship trophy were especially rewarding.

City champions under coaches Marg Kavanagh and Ester Shatz. School Archives photo

Coach Jack Lansdell and girls volleyball team (1982-'83) with the late Mrs. Judy Bourne, volleyball guru for Victoria schoolchildren. School Archives photo

During the 1980s under the direction of principal Garnet Jackson, and vice principal Ken MacCaskel, students strived to do things "the George Jay way", by practising the three Cs - courtesy, co-operation, and consideration. Certain youngsters would require the odd reminder of course, but generally students would apply themselves. As always, good motivation would ensure good mileage. Principal Jackson had to smile the day the irate neighbor came into the office to complain about young fellows who had stolen grapes from his garden at noon hour on their way back to school. Teacher Mr. Gretsinger (fondly referred to as Mr. G. by the students) who

Robert DeMilo in action on Mr. Lansdell's City Championship Team (School Archives Photo)

The library is home to the popular "Read for the Top" contest begun in 1983. School Archives photo

happened to be in the office at the time said the scene reminded him of the title of John Steinbeck's novel "The Grapes of Wrath".

Occasional events served to remind one that George Jay was an inner city school in a growing urban area. One such event was the arrival of the Victoria City Police S.W.A.T. Team to investigate an adult who was carrying a weapon. Another incident was the early morning deposit of a suitcase of drugs on the school steps following a robbery at a nearby drug store. Teachers arrived at work to find city detectives already on the job.

Principal Jackson did his detective work the weekend one of his young students had been handing out $100 bills to his friends. It seemed the youngster had found money the parents had been saving to send to relatives in the 'old country'. Most of the money was retrieved but a couple of youngsters had an enjoyable weekend. Police officers were not impressed the time they were called to check on the story of an attempted abduction. Three young fellows, after an extended lunch hour, and in an attempt to cover their absense, made up the story of a white van and driver who had attempted to entice them into the van. Police soon got to the truth of the matter and the young truants realized the seriousness of their fictious story. I'm sure many principals could write a book of their own.

A highlight of the school year for senior students is the annual trip to camp Columbia on nearby Thetis Island. Students plan and fund raise all year for the fun filled three or four days at camp. The trips were begun in the 1980s when teachers Ms. M. Kavanagh and Mrs. A. Nilsen wanted the students to experience the typical summer time games and activities that go along with camping. The Camp Columbia trips have evolved into an experience filled with opportunity for marine and nature study, water safety and boating, camp crafts and many other camping activities. Many a student reflects back with fond memories of their days at camp with the grade sevens. The 1980s ended with principal Bob Tubman at the helm. His caring, compassionate manner helped students steer a steady course and they would continue to learn in an atmosphere of courtesy, co-operation and consideration.

Teacher Barb Tarbot and 'friend' kick off the "Walk, Jog, Run," fitness program for students. (School Archives Photo)

Touch the Future - the 1990s

"I touch the future - I teach."

- Christa McAuliffe - American teacher and astronaut

For George Jay School, the 1990s were a decade of great strides in terms of overall accomplishment lead by strong administrative teams. A report at a staff meeting in the 1990s may have come from groups not heard of 10 or 20 years ago; for example, the Technology committee, the Inner City committee, the Opportunity Room, the Parents Room, the Greening committee, and so on...

The schools of the 1990s were different than ever before. Society had changed. The decade began in an aura of optimism. The 1980s had ended with the Royal Commission on Education of 1988. Premier Vander Zalm's election promise had been carried out and lead to enthusiasm and excitement in the educational community when all but 2 of the 83 recommendations of the commission were carried out. The 'Year 2000' program provided a framework for reform. The program was to be short lived - public opposition probably led to N.D.P. Premier Mike Harcourt's announcement of the end of the program, although " many individual teachers, schools, and districts are using year 2000 - type programs and techniques because they feel that the principles work."[1]

1 p. 7 School Yard Bullies

George Jay Staff - 1992 (School Archives Photo)

In November of 1993 the Ministry of Education presented changes to B.C.'s education policy with the document "Improving the Quality of Education in British Columbia". The document presented by the Honorable Minister, Art Charbonneau, pointed out that recent successful changes to the school system would be maintained, built upon and strengthened. Basic skills are emphasized to prepare children to become literate, informed and responsible citizens.

"Ensuring that students learn to read, write and do basic mathematics is a primary goal of schools. These traditional basics are at the centre of an expanded set of essential skills that students need in today's world. The most important of these are the ability to solve problems and to use computer-based technology."[2]

We know social factors affect the way the children learn. Many factors have changed a great deal in the last few years - most importantly; the economy, ethnic heritage and family structure. The recession of the early 1990s and resulting unemployment and low income for many has resulted in changes in our schools. The ethnic diversity of our schools is growing. This is most noted in our larger cities. More than 50% of the students in the

2 "Improving the Quality of Education in British Columbia," Nov. 1993. Ministry of Education.

The busy computer lab adjacent to the library-resource centre
B. Gretsinger photo

Ms. Doherty's ukulele class.
B. Gretsinger photo 1997

Vancouver school district speak English as a second language. If George Jay school was representative of the schools in Victoria then the capital city of our province would not be far behind Vancouver in terms of number of students speaking a foreign language. With a high percentage of the George Jay students speaking English as a second language and over 30 different languages and dialects being spoken by families of students in the school , it is easy to see the rich cultural diversity. To see the classroom bulletin boards with the world maps and indicators of student origins is most interesting. What potential for a stimulating, sharing, learning environment.

Teacher Maureen Lennie and class on an October visit to Goldstream Park to view the spawning salmon. (School Archives Photo)

We know parental involvement helps students succeed. Today, fewer parents have as much time as they would like, to become involved in their child's education. Statistics show more families have both parents working than 10 or 20 years ago, and more families have only one parent. The involvement and commitment of the school parent group is all the more remarkable when we note that 40% of the students are from single parent families.

In 1991 the Honorable Anita Hagen, Minister of Education, introduced the School Meals Program to the province. Parents at "inner city" schools now had the opportunity to have their children receive a meal at lunchtime, five days a week. At George Jay, two thirds, to three quarters of the 350 students take part in the lunch program. Under the direction of Anne Crozier-Smith and Pat Hansen, six student helpers at two stations serve some 250

Students under A. Crozier-Smith & P.Hansen serve some 250 lunches daily.
B.Gretsinger photo 1997

lunches daily within a 15 to 20 minute time span and students have the opportunity to go back for seconds. Four of the five meals each week are served hot. Bagged lunches are made available for classes going on field trips. Nutritionists work on the menus and portions to ensure healthy, balanced meals. On a cold winter day, it gives one a good feeling to see the trays with hot lunches being carefully carried down the hallway to classrooms by young students you just know are going to enjoy their meals. "In 1997 the cost of the Victoria program was $1.2 million. Province wide, the meal program served 345 schools at a cost of $15 million. That's up considerably from 1991-92, when fewer than 60 schools were served with a budget of only $2.5 million."[3]

Students who arrive at school in the morning and may have missed breakfast are able to get a bite to eat by stopping off at the toast club. Staff, students and volunteers make and serve as much toast and jam or peanut butter as is needed. It is difficult to imagine students trying to do their best on an empty stomach.

---

3 Victoria Times Colonist, Oct. 8, 1997 p. A3

In 1993 the Inner City Schools program was introduced by the Ministry of Education. George Jay was one of the first schools in Victoria to receive extra funding under the new program. In actual fact; the need was shown, and funding for George Jay was among the highest in the province. Funded under this new program was the 'Opportunity Room', under the direction of Mrs. Kathy Spiller, which filled a real need for students having problems other than academics. Along the same line, the 'Second Step' program that Mrs. Spiller and staff use, helps youngsters deal with social problems and develop life skills. Funding from the Inner City program also helps with field trips for classes and to bring drama, music, and art programs into the school, all of which helps to 'level the playing field' these students are on. Principal Brian Wile was a strong advocate of students from a "have not area" being given an equal opportunity in their educational development, thus the effort and energy put into the successful application for 'Inner City funding'.

The 'parent room' at George Jay Elementary is extremely successful and is a model for other schools in the district. Parental involvement is greater than ever before in the history of the school. The school has opened its' doors to the community. There are now over one hundred volunteers taking an active part in the day to day programs of the school.The 'parent room' is part of the reason. According to an article in the Victoria Times Colonist newspaper entitled 'Program helps parents become better students,' "the inner-city school's unique parents resource room is the creation of Tessa Lloyd, a child and family counsellor on contract to the Greater Victoria School District, who wants to make education a happy experience for the school's kids - and for their parents".[4]

The "parent room" at George Jay School is a model for other schools in the district.

The parents are an active part of all that's going on. The parents run a "safe arrival" program and check by phone each morning with any parents when youngsters fail to arrive at school on time and there has been no notice to the school that they would be absent. They support teachers by finding drivers for field trips or extra support for special activities. The school's chess club under volunteers Jack Jeffrey and Tim Bethel is as good as any in the province. Our young chess players provide a challenge to the students of neighboring Victoria High School. The parent advisory committee or P.A.C. is a very dedicated group. This pattern of parental involvement would be typical for every school in the province that is working the way it was meant to be. Family dances, craft fairs, bake sales etc. all help to raise funds that are used in all areas of the school. Rewards are garnered

4 Times Colonist, June 13, 1996

Parent's Resource Room - a model for other schools in the district.
B. Gretsinger photo 1997

in all areas when the teacher-student-parent relationship becomes a partnership for education.

The annual corn roast, introduced in the early '90s, and held during the first few weeks back to school has evolved into a fun 'meet the teacher' night. Staff prepare and serve hot dogs and freshly picked corn to some 600 to 700 parents and students, as well as many former students - a great 'kick-off' to the school year.

The administrative teams of the 1990s have played a big part in having the school be what it is today. Under principal Brian Wile, who was nominated by staff for the national 'Excellence in Education' award, the Inner City schools funding began to play a part in daily operations. Programs and projects came together that would interest and motivate students. The old washroom that was converted into a photography development lab under the direction of teacher Bob Gretsinger got many students interested in an area of learning that not many elementary schools can offer to their students. Vice principal Santosh Clarke played a strong role in these formative years before moving on to her first principalship at Hampton Elementary school. In 1994 , the new principal to Victoria from Burnaby, Mrs. Mary Hendy, continued the strong leadership role at George Jay. Mrs. Hendy's English background added a pleasant, refreshing note to the school and her desire to put the students first and meet their needs endeared her to the staff. The fine arts

Div. 16 - 1993-1994 School Learning Assistance Teacher - Leona Winstone, Class Teacher -Maureen Lennie, Teaching Assistants - Pat Hansen & Carole Hester

Strong administrative teams - important for the 1990s.: Principal Mary Hendy and Vice Principal Gary Glover B. Gretsinger photos 1997

received a 'booster shot' from new vice principal Lynne Moorhouse during her short tenure in administration before moving on to a new principalship at Sundance elementary school. The addition to staff in 1996 of vice principal Gary Glover insured that the trend of strong administrative teams would continue.

We hear and read of numerous reports, studies, or surveys, that tell us or indicate that public school education is failing, or is not getting its' moneys worth, or worse still, is in a state of chaos. There are schools out there that are an effective community enterprise where education is working well. These good schools are made; they hum with a productive energy. Characteristics of a good school include:

- leadership which models high standards of professional conduct and puts the school and children first.
- good teachers dedicated to the welfare and learning of students.
- a focus on teaching and learning while concentrating on mastery of reading, writing, and mathematics.
- accountability to students and parents.
- shared responsibility by administration, staff, students, and parents.

The Mission Statement of the school states that:

"George Jay School, in partnership with the parents, will work to enable the pupils to develop their maximum intellectual potential to foster in each pupil a sense of self-worth, the worth of fellow pupils, and to develop a sense of social responsibility. This will be done in an environment that is safe, flexible, caring and responsive to individual needs."

In 1997 the School Meals Program served 345 schools in the province at a cost of $15 million.

These are lofty goals, and as in all businesses, some days are better than others; but when that hum of productive energy settles over the old building it gives one a good feeling and a sense we're on the right track.

A building can only be as good as the people within: staff and students and the community make a school. Dedicated, caring staff coupled with strong administration and willing, working parents makes for a winning combination.

Interests and passions, whatever they may be, are reflected throughout a teaching career. Primary teacher Syd Langhelt, for example, has always had a special interest in professional development for teachers. Over his thirty six years of teaching he has spent thousands of hours working on professional development at the school, the district, and the provincial level. It is this kind of dedication to an area like "Pro. D." that enriches the careers of so many colleagues. Teacher Don Jones has a passion for sailing which might be noticed when the unit he is teaching involves using the program of study - 'The Voyage of the Mimi'. Don, with the help of teaching assistant Stan Purves, even had his special class

Science in action. Launching rockets to finish a unit of study on 'Space Exploration'. Entire student body helping with countdowns.
(B.Gretsinger photo - 1996)

build a twelve foot sailboat in the classroom over the course of the school year. This kind of project involves a tremendous amount of extra work, but enables the students to have a learning experience they'll remember for many years.

Boat building - A special project for a special class (D. Jones Photo)

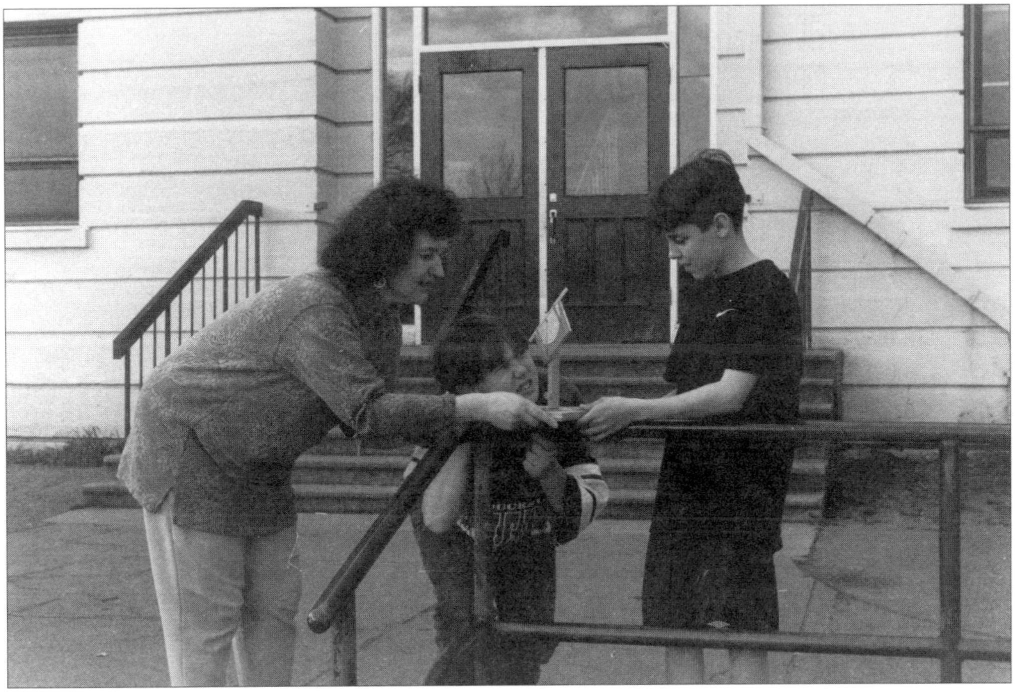

Teacher Anne Nilsen with students Mathias and Cory learning to use their home made astrolabes to find the azimuth of a body in space. (B.Gretsinger Photo - 1998)

Teacher Anne Nilsen's interest in astronomy has resulted in students doing wonderful units of study as part of their science work. Nighttime class visits to the local Dominion Astrophysical Observatory in neighboring Saanich enable her classes to really take a "hands on" approach to their lessons.

Teacher Bob Gretsinger's interest in mechanics lead to the development of a unit of study whereby each student in the class built their own electric motor. Throughout the province exciting locally developed lessons and units of study enrich the work of many students. The more teachers are able to share these ideas, the more students benefit.

Mike Crawley in his book Schoolyard Bullies says we must co-operate as we try to find answers while striving to achieve what's best for kids.

"Teachers need to be more flexible in dealing with the uniqueness of each child. Unions need to consider the best interests of kids, not just their members. Politicians need to show courage and vision and stand up for public education, not just for what's popular. Bureaucrats must be willing to allow more humanity into the system. Each parent must remember that although his or her child is important, the school is there for the benefit of all. And we as a society must examine what we're asking when we demand something from the schools to ensure our demands don't get in the way of what's best for kids."

Winners of the 1998 "Read for the Top" contest, (left to right: Jessica Neal, Stephanie Woolrich, Sheralyn Madam, & Nyre Murphy) with Canada's premier writer for children and young adults, Eric Wilson, and friend/agent Flo Connolly. (B. Gretsinger photo - May, 1998).

Mr. Crawley states the school system is not perfect, nor is it in crisis. The truth lies somewhere between the two extremes: the schools could do with some improvement.

Education is a team game and when all players have the same goal in mind success can only be the result.

As we approach the 21st century we know there will be changes down the road, as change is part of the history of education. Some things will remain the same. Good teachers will still encourage their students to reach goals and while striving for excellence they will set standards and challenge the students to reach them. As far as George Jay School is concerned, principal Mary Hendy says, "the direction of the school is set for the future. George Jay is an integral part of the community and it is as a part of that community that the school will continue to thrive."

The direction may include George Jay Elementary and neighboring Central Junior High and Victoria High School all becoming community schools, which would enable more community participation and greater integration of all the services that are provided. By planning together for the needs of the Fernwood Area, the three schools, the Community Recreation Center, and the Community Association would be better able to utilize all the resources of the neighborhood, including school facilities.

The social committee of the school is only a small part of the whole but it helps with the overall well being; the comraderie, and the good humour, which all play a part of a successful working, learning environment. The untidy staff room which is cleaned by staff on a weekly rotation soon became neater when staff humor guru, Mr. Gretsinger mounted a video camera above the sink. Using an old barbecue rotisserie, the old camera actually panned the staff room when plugged in. Lots of laughs were shared and even more followed when a staged video was shown at the next staff meeting .The year end luncheons the social committee plans for the staff on the last day of June have everyone leaving on a high note ready for a good holiday and a well earned rest. Many remember the year the afternoon began with the comment: "Usually we give gifts to those leaving ," and then the social committee proceeded to give gifts all nicely wrapped to all those staff who were returning next year. If a good laugh is healthy then many benefited the year the belly dancer arrived at the staff luncheon looking for the two Bobs to help entertain - a departing gift from vice principal Lynne Moorhouse. Gifts for those leaving may be somewhat silly but good laughs are shared by all. If laughter rings in the hallways,chances are your school is a happy, healthy place to learn.

There are over 100 volunteers taking an active part in the day to day programs of the school.

George Jay Staff June, 1998

Bibliography

1. Annual Reports of the Public Schools of the Province of B.C. 1909-1910, 1911-1912, 1917-1918, 1950-1985.
- Report on the building of Victoria's schools.
- Annual Report of the Board of School Trustees.- 1911, 1912

2. Come Give A Cheer - One Hundred Years of Victoria High School 1876 - 1976 Peter L, Smith

3. The Fernwood Files, by John J. Ellis; 1989 Orca Book Publishers

4. "Glancing Back" Reflections and Anecdotes on the History of Vancouver's Public Schools. Edited by Chuck Gosbee and Leslie Dyson. Vanc. School Board.

5. Grading the Teacher, by Nellie Jacobs. Penguin Books, 1996

6. A History of Public Education in B.C. Johnson, F.Henry; U.B.C. Vanc. 1964

7. "Improving the Quality of Education in British Columbia." November 1993.-British Columbia Ministry of Education

8. A Legacy for Learners. The Report of the Royal Commission on Education. 1988

9. Schooling and Society in 20th Century British Columbia. Edited by J. Donald Wilson, David C. Jones. Detselig Enterprises Ltd. Calgary, Alberta c.1980

10. School's Out. by Andrew Nikiforuk; 1993 Macfarlane, Walter & Ross; Toronto,

11. Schoolyard Bullies, by Mike Crawley; 1995 Orca Book Publishers.

12. Vancouver Province Newspaper

13. Victoria Daily Colonist Newspaper

14. Victoria Times Newspaper

15. Victoria Times Colonist Newspaper

Reunion

Autographs